Spiritual Marketing

A Proven 5-Step Formula for Easily Creating Wealth from the Inside Out

by Joe Vitale

Foreword by Bob Proctor

© 2002 by Joe Vitale

All rights reserved.
No part of this book may be reproduced, stored in a retrieval
system, or transmitted by any means, electronic, mechanical,
photocopying, recording, or otherwise, without written
permission from the author.

ISBN: 0-7596-1431-8

This book is printed on acid free paper.

1stBooks rev. 3/5/02

"Spirit is substance which forms itself according to
your demands, and must have a pattern from which to
work. A pan of dough is as willing to be formed into bread
as biscuit. It makes as little difference to Spirit
what we demand."

-- Frances Larimer Warner,
Our Invisible Supply: Part One, 1907

This publication is designed to provide accurate information in regard to the subject matter covered. It is offered with the understanding that the author and publisher are not engaged in rendering medical or psychological service. This book is not intended to be a substitute for therapy or professional advice.

Acknowledgments

I am grateful to Jerry and Esther Hicks for their insights into the process of creating whatever you want. I am of course grateful to Jonathan Jacobs for his work as a healer, miracles coach, and friend. I am also grateful for Bill Ferguson's magic. Linda Credeur was the first to believe in this project, maybe even before me. I want to thank Bob Proctor, an enlightened businessman awakening people wherever he goes, for his support and belief in me as well as this book. A few special friends read early versions of this material and gave me priceless feedback. They deserve a round of applause: Jonathan Morningstar, Jennifer Wier, Blair Warren, David Deutsch, Bryan Miller, Nerissa Oden, Rick and Mary Barrett. Marian, of course, has been the sunshine in my life for more than two decades now. I am forever grateful for having her in my world. Finally, I am grateful for the Spirit of life for guiding me in every moment.

For Bonnie

About the Author

Joe Vitale, the creator of Spiritual Marketing, is an independent marketing specialist currently based in Austin, Texas. His talks, seminars, and audiotape programs on sales and marketing have helped thousands of people around the globe market their businesses successfully. Among Joe's clients are Doubleday Books, the American Business Women's Association, PBS Television, and the American Red Cross. He is the author of ten books, including "The Seven Lost Secrets of Success" and "There's A Customer Born Every Minute." He's also the author of an audiotape program for Nightingale-Conant, called "The Power of Outrageous Marketing!"

Joe Vitale

e-mail: *spirit@mrfire.com* * website:

http://www.mrfire.com

Table of Contents

Miracles Never Stop

Preface to the 1stbooks.com Edition

I wrote most of what you are about to read in 1999, when I first issued this book as a private gift to only 35 people. More miracles have happened since then. Here are a few of them:

* When I first wrote this book and described the car of my dreams, the car of my dreams at that time was a Saturn. I've now upgraded my dream and my car. I'm now driving a BMW Z3 2.8 Roadster. I've never in my life had so much fun driving!!! As I grew in my life, and became more bold about going for my dreams, I also naturally wanted a different vehicle. I was led to the Z3, which symbolizes the major changes in my life. And it is a hoot to drive, as well! You truly can have anything you can imagine.

* When I first wrote this book, I was still married to Marian, who I had been with for more than twenty years. Since then we decided we had grown apart. There was nothing negative about the experience or the decision at all.

Marian decided she preferred being alone. I decided to look for another partner. I found one, too, in Nerissa, who I am deeply in love with. I'm still friends with Marian, and both are now in my heart. I'm a lucky man. Major changes in life can truly be easy and effortless.

* When I first wrote this book, I made a goal that I wanted passive income. I wanted money to come to me easily and effortlessly, always, consistently, no matter where I was or what I was doing. I was then led to meet Mark Joyner, CEO of Aesop Marketing, who asked if he could put one of my books online as an e-book. I was skeptical. But I gave him "Hypnotic Writing," a manuscript I wrote many years ago. Mark put it online, marketed it, and the sales blew my socks off. Even now, seven months after the book went online at http://www.Hypnotic Writing.com, orders keep coming in. Since there is no book to print, stock, or mail, all the money is passive income. Every month I receive a check, sometimes for staggering amounts. Now I smile a lot. I know that when you set an intention, you set the forces of life to bring it to you, and you to it.

* When I first wrote this book, I was living in Houston. After I met Nerissa, I moved to Austin. I then began the process of manifesting our dream home. After a few months, we found a beautiful two-acre, two-story, Hill Country property with wandering wild deer and rabbit, and an outside pool, between Austin and San Antonio, in a small spiritual-artistic community called Wimberley, Texas. Finding this home was a matter of having a clear image of what I wanted while following every intuitive impulse I had. The result was a miracle.

I just sat down with Nerissa and talked to her about the on-going miracles in my life.

"It happens to you all the time," she said.

She mentioned that just the other day I wanted to book us a flight to Ohio to see my family. Tickets were nearly one thousand dollars. I simply expected to get a better deal while being willing to accept the going fare. When I called the airline back, they told me I had enough frequent flyer miles to get both tickets for just over one hundred dollars. Way cool.

And Nerissa reminded me of the time I wanted to complete my collection of rare books by P.T. Barnum. I

Joe Vitale

found the last book needed. But my intuition said not to pay the high price the book seller was asking. I let go. I waited. A few days later the book seller lowered his price. That's almost unheard of. And yes, I bought the book.

And she reminded me of the time I looked for one book for nearly seven years and couldn't find it. Then, out of the blue, an email friend in Canada wrote me that he had the book. I begged to buy it. He declined. But a few days later he suddenly decided to just send me the book---at no charge!

And she remembered that a year or so ago, when I couldn't find a friend of mine that I loved and missed, I gave up and hired a private investigator. He couldn't find my friend, either. But then one day, simply following my intuition, I walked right up to my friend at a yoga class. I found her without breaking a sweat.

Nerissa also reminded me to to tell you what happened just yesterday, while writing this very preface.

I have been practicing the Sedona Method for months now. It's a very simple method for releasing any emotion or negative experience in the way of your being happy right now. I like the method and have told many people about it through my monthly e-newsletter.

I was reading a book by Lester Levenson, the founder of the Sedona Method, just yesterday morning. I sat in my easy chair, reading, feeling happy, wondering how I might learn more about Sedona and Lester. I remember thinking, "Gee, it sure would be nice to meet some Sedona people and learn more about what they do."

That same day I checked my email and to my delighted surprise, there was a message from the director of the Sedona Institute. He had heard about me through the grapevine and wanted to talk to me about how I could help promote their website at http://www.sedona.com. Wow!

And then there are the countless times when I want more money for something or other, and I get a brainstorm that pulls in an abundance of money fast.

One time I almost led a seminar on "Spiritual Marketing." Instead, I decided to see if anyone would sign up for it online and take it as an e-class. I announced that the class would only be done by email, would only last five weeks, and would cost $1,500 per person. Fifteen people signed up, bringing me a whopping sum of money in just a short period of time. Very nice.

"You have miracles happen all the time," Nerissa repeated.

"Why do you think that is?" I asked her. "It certainly wasn't always like that."

"Because you now practice the Spiritual Marketing steps," she explained. "You make yourself a magnet for whatever you want."

There's no question about it. If I tried to document all the miracles that keep occurring in just my life alone because of the "Spiritual Marketing" method, I'd never stop writing this book and never get around to releasing it to the public.

My point is this: The five step formula you are about to discover works.

And because it works, I want you to have it.

I once told Nerissa that there is an easy path through life and a hard path. When I first met her, she was crawling up the rocky side of the mountain. I pointed out that there is an escalator through life, too. You can take the hard path or the easy path. It's all your choice.

This book shows you where the escalator is located.

Get on it and enjoy the ride.

I'm going to turn off my computer now, turn this book over to 1stbooks.com, and let you read it.

Let me know what you think...and what miracles then occur in your life, too.

Joe Vitale

spirit@mrfire.com

"If we don't like what's happening to us in the world, all we have to do is change our consciousness---and the world out there changes for us!"

-- Lester Levenson, "*Keys to the Ultimate Freedom,*" 1993

Foreword by Bob Proctor

I opened the Fed-X package and found a spiral bound manuscript inside. Two words jumped off the cover: Spiritual Marketing. Hmmm. Is that ever an interesting title, I thought to myself. Those two words...Spiritual Marketing...kept waltzing around in my mind.

I never before looked at those two words as partners, but there they were side by side in perfect harmony. What a beautiful couple they made. They definitely belong together. Yes, the marrying of these two words has created the potential to cause a profound, positive impact upon the world....yours as well as mine. From somewhere inside the thought came to me that it would take a Joe Vitale to create such a powerful combination. I also thought, Joe is not only a great guy, he writes great books.

You are very likely as anxious to get into this book as I was when I first got it in my hands. However, before you wander any further, an important clarification must be established:

By "Spiritual Marketing," we do not mean religious marketing. The author of this dynamite little book and I are in full agreement that neither one of us are remotely qualified to write on that subject. We are instead referring to the presence within of the universal spirit...the true self.

Spirit is present and operates in everything. Spirit always expresses itself perfectly...by Law. The best definition of the word "law" that I have ever found in my close to forty years of fun-filled research came from Dr. Thurman Fleet. He explained, "Law is the uniform and orderly method of the omnipotent God."

As you read any of Joe Vitale's books or listen to any of his recorded programs, you will realize he loves studying the Laws. In this, his most recent book, Joe has effectively married the Laws with his other true love, marketing. You and I are the beneficiaries of his years of work. He has taken what can be a very complex, laborious task and delivered it in just five simple seps. The five steps outlined in Spiritual Marketing will help you accomplish or acquire anything you seriously desire. I know this to be true because I have personally used these five steps for the last forty years to establish and reach numerous goals all over the world.

Although you will find each step easy to understand, following them will require discipline. Your old paradigm, which is more commonly referred to as your "old conditioning," will fight you. In fact, your old conditioning may put up a tremendous battle.

Paradigms definitely do not die easily and the weapons the paradigms use to hold you back in life have awesome potential power. I often refer to them as the trio that have the power to paralyze....that are in fact insidious. They are DOUBT, FEAR, and ANXIETY. They have the power to bring your progress to an abrupt halt right at the point you are making the decision to make your move.

You must realize that the doubt creeps in and causes the fear, which in turn then causes the anxiety. The three can strike at lightening speed. However, they can and must be stopped. The primary cause of these debilitating demons is IGNORANCE.

Know the truth and the truth will set you free. That in itself is a beautiful truth. You must understand that there is only one thing to be set free from and that is ignorance. The second you feel doubt creeping into your mind, pick up this little book and read a few pages. Open it anywhere and read. Wonderful things will begin to happen. Your enthusiasm will soar and you will be back on the right road to a bright future.

This little book will become your friend, your own personal Aladdin's Lamp. The concepts on each page will strengthen you. Don't leave home without it!

Every now and then when you are reading, stop reading, lay your book down, sit back in a relaxed state and think. Think of some wealthy, well-balanced people you know....think of what they have been doing with their lives...and you will suddenly realize they are doing what this little book is suggesting you do.

Who are some of the biggest producers in your industry? Think! They are doing what this book suggests you do!

Now proceed to Step One. Turn each and every step into a habitual part of your behavior. Read this book every day. As you do, you will begin to enjoy the progressive realization of all your heart's desires!

-- Bob Proctor

Toronto

Author's True Confession

I admit it.

I never wanted to publish this book or make it available to a wide audience.

I was scared.

I wrote this book for one person: My sister. Bonnie had three kids, was unemployed, and was on welfare. It hurt me to see her suffer. I knew her life could be different if she knew the five step process I developed for creating whatever she wanted. I wrote this material for her, and only for her, in 1997. She's now off welfare and doing fine. She's not rich yet, but I think I've shown her a new way to live life.

I never wanted to make this book public because I was nervous about how the world would perceive me. I've written ten books so far, for such well known and conservative organizations as the American Marketing Association and the American Management Association. I also have an audiotape program with Nightingale-Conant. I figured if I told the world about my interest in spirituality, people would ridicule me, clients would fire me, and these e Vitale_

organizations would shun me. So I played it safe and kept this book a secret.

But in June, 1999 I felt the inner urge to give a copy of the manuscript to this book to Bob Proctor, at the beginning of one of his Science of Getting Rich seminars. Bob read it and loved it. And then he did something shocking.

There were 250 people in that seminar in Denver. Bob stood before them and read off all of my book titles, and then introduced me to the crowd. I stood and the crowd applauded. They treated me like a celebrity and I loved the attention.

But then Bob told everyone about my new book, my unpublished book, about this book. I was surprised. I wasn't ready for this. I held my breath. And then Bob told them the title to it: Spiritual Marketing.

There was such a hush throughout the crowd that chills went up my spine. Not only did people favorably react to the book, but they all wanted it, and now. At least fifty people came up and said they wanted to buy the book. Bob Proctor later said he wanted to record it. And one publisher in the seminar said he wanted to publish the book, sight unseen!

My concerns about publishing this book vanished. I could see that the timing was right to release these ideas, and I saw that I would be safe in doing so.

So here I am.

As with most things in life, there's little to be afraid of and wealth and glory await right around the corner. All you have to do is step forward and do the things you're being nudged from within to do.

Bob Proctor nudged me in front of 250 people.

And this book is the result.

Enjoy it--and live long and prosper!

-- Joe Vitale

Austin

How I Created Spiritual Marketing

"What do you do?" I asked.

I was standing in a line of 700 people in a hotel in Seattle, waiting to spend a day listening to an author and spiritual teacher.

"I do energy work," the woman beside me replied. "It's hard to explain. It's different for each person."

"Do you have a business card?"

"No," she said, slightly embarrassed.

I was shocked.

"Let me ask you a question," I began. "There are over 700 potential clients here for you. Why don't you at least have business cards?"

A woman beside her smiled and told her, "You were just hit by an angel."

I'm not an angel. But I was curious why this business woman was missing a huge marketing opportunity. As I talked to a few more of the 700 people at this event, I realized all of these people were in business for themselves. And they all needed help in marketing themselves.

That's when it dawned on me that I could write a concise handbook on spiritually based marketing. No one else seemed better qualified. I'm the author of *The AMA Complete Guide to Small Business Advertising* for The American Marketing Association, and I have over fifteen years of experience in metaphysics and spirituality. I've interviewed many new age spokespeople and have had some of them as my clients. Besides, I had already created and tested a secret five-step process for manifesting anything you wanted. I seemed like the best voice for a book on marketing with spirit.

I also knew that those 700 people at the seminar represented a still larger group of people who need help with their businesses. I further knew that they were all doing something inside themselves that was creating their outer results. In other words, their inner state of being was creating their business, or lack of it.

Said more simply, the woman who didn't have a business card had an inner insecurity about her business that showed up in her life by her not having business cards. And taking this logic a step further in the direction I want to take you later in this book, if that woman were truly clear about her business, she wouldn't even need business cards. Business would just come to her. Her inner spirit would do her marketing.

That's what this book will reveal. I've learned that we are human beings, not human doings. When you reach a clear inner state of being about your service to the world, the world will come to you. As one successful person said, "Angels now hand out my business cards." Confused? That's okay. Therapist, author and my dear friend Mandy Evans says confusion is that wonderful state of mind right before clarity.

Maybe the following story will give you a glimpse of what I'm talking about and set the stage for what is to follow:

I once read a delightful old book from 1920 titled *Fundamentals of Prosperity* by Roger Babson. He ended his book by asking the President of the Argentine Republic why South America, with all of its natural resources and wonders, was so far behind North America in terms of progress and marketing. The President replied:

"I have come to this conclusion. South America was settled by the Spanish who came to South America in search of gold, but North America was settled by the Pilgrim Fathers who went there in search of God."

Where is your focus? On money or on spirit?

In this book I intend to offer a new way for you to easily and effortlessly increase your business. It's based on proven marketing techniques and timeless spiritual principles. It will reveal how your inner state of being attracts and creates your outer results---and what to do about it so you can have, do, or be whatever your heart desires.

Do the techniques work? The proof will be in the pudding. Try them and see. I can tell you about the successes I've had---and I do in this book---but nothing will be quite as convincing to you as using these simple ideas and seeing your own amazing results. I could tell you that this method will help you manifest anything you want. You'll read about people who created cars and homes, healed themselves of cancer, and created new relationships. But I'm focusing on business because there appears to be a serious lack of spirituality in business. And I'm going to let you discover the magic of marketing with spirit because nothing will be more powerful as your own first hand experiences.

Pull up a chair. Get comfortable. Take a deep breath. Relax. Let's talk about how you can increase your business---and achieve anything else you may desire---through the magic power of "Spiritual Marketing."

"Living at risk is jumping off the cliff and building your wings on the way down."

-- Ray Bradbury

It Can Be Another Way....

Before I became a marketing specialist and author, I was an inner world journalist for over ten years, writing for several leading edge magazines. As a result, I've seen miracles with my own eyes. For example:

* I interviewed Meir Schneider, a man who was diagnosed as blind. He was given a certificate saying he was incurably blind, and yet today he sees, he reads, he writes, he drives a car---and he has helped hundreds of people regain their vision, as well.

* I spent time with Barry and Suzi Kaufman at their Option Institute and saw and heard of miracles there. Their own child was born autistic. They were told to give up on him. But they didn't. They worked with their son, loved him, nurtured him, accepted him---and healed him. Today he lives as an above average, happy, successful adult.

* I've sat in dozens of workshops where I saw people heal their relationships with their lovers, their parents, their kids. I've interviewed gurus and mentors, talked to people who have had "incurable" problems dissolved, and I've experienced miracles first-hand in my own life. I've come to believe that nothing---nothing!---is impossible.

Recently I've been working with Jonathan Jacobs, a man called "the healer's healer" because his track record for helping heal people is so stunning that doctors are referring their own patients to him. I've seen Jonathan take people with everything from money problems to back injuries to cancer, and help heal them, often in a single session.

I've tasted this myself. For most of my life I struggled with money. When I lived in Dallas some twenty years ago, I was homeless and starving. I shoplifted to eat. And when I moved to Houston, I found it a frustrating nightmare to come up with $200 a month to live in a dump. It was hell. Yet I went through it for nearly fifteen years. YEARS!

Then, after doing a few sessions with Jonathan, I somehow let go of my old beliefs about money, installed new ones, and now my finances are so amazingly different that I am often in awe that I have so much: new cars, new home, world travel, more clients than I can handle, and a constant stream of cash that keeps me above water at all times. I pay every bill that arrives, when it arrives, and I never experience lack.

What happened? How can Meir cure the blind? The Kaufmans heal autism? Jonathan help people with any list of problems? Me have money when for a decade I had next to none?

It begins with knowing that "It can be another way." That's what I want you to understand right now. That no matter what is happening in your life, no matter what you think will happen, it can be another way. The direction you appear to be headed can be altered. Nothing is set in concrete.

In fact, as you'll see, everything in life seems to be plastic. You can mold it to fit what you want and where you want to go. Even right now, as you read these words, you can begin to play with new possibilities: What do you want to be, do, or have? Win the lotto? Why not? Increase your business? Why not? Heal something? Why not?

A friend of mine asked, "How do you know what is impossible?"

I replied, "How do you know what isn't?"

I believe our planet is what was described in a Star Trek television episode called "Shore Leave." When Kirk and his team land on a planet to check it out before sending the rest of the crew down for some much needed rest and relaxation, they begin to experience odd events. McCoy sees a huge white rabbit. Sulu sees an ancient samurai who chases him. Kirk sees an old lover and an old classmate. After experiencing the joys and sorrows of these events, it finally dawns on the crew (thanks to Spock, of course) that they are on a planet that reads their thoughts and creates what they think about.

I think Earth is that planet. What you hold in your mind with energy and focus will tend to be created in your reality. It takes a little longer to experience results because we keep changing our minds. Imagine going to a restaurant and ordering chicken soup. But before it arrives you change your order to won ton soup. And before that arrives you change your order back to chicken soup. You'll sit there and complain, saying "I can never get what I want!", when in reality you are the reason your soup is late!

Most of us do that every day. Our indecision makes manifesting what we want nearly impossible. No wonder you end up feeling that you can't get what you want. Yet, it doesn't have to be that way.

Consider what Frances Larimer Warner wrote in *Our Invisible Supply: Part One*, in 1907:

"Spirit is substance which forms itself according to your demands, and must have a pattern from which to work. A pan of dough is as willing to be formed into bread as biscuit. It makes as little difference to Spirit what we demand."

That's the foundation to the five-step process I'll describe in this book: Knowing that life can be different for you, and that life itself will support you in what you want.

Here's how:

"Try to remember that the picture you think, feel and see is reflected into the Universal Mind, and by the natural law of reciprocal action must return to you in either spiritual or physical form."

-- *Your Invisible Power* by Genevieve Behrend, 1921

Step One:
Know what you don't want.

Do I need to explain this one?

Most people I talk to every day know what they don't want. "I don't want this back ache." "I don't want this headache." "I don't want these bills." "I don't want to struggle in my business." You know the list. You have one of your own.

Unfortunately, that's where most of us leave it. The nature of our conversations, our newspaper reporting, our radio and television shows, and our popular talk shows surround the idea of what we don't want. It feels good to complain. We don't feel so alone. We feel heard. We feel relieved. We even sometimes get answers that make our problems lighter.

But we seldom take this process to level two. It's a rare person who will stop complaining or fighting long enough to focus on the opposite of what they are experiencing. Yet, level two begins to bring on the miracles and manifestations that we want. Knowing what you don't want is the springboard to your miracles. Knowing what you don't want is simply your current reality.

And current reality can change.

"Man is a magnet, and every line and dot and detail of his experiences come by his own attraction."

-- *The Life Power and How To Use It*, by Elizabeth Towne, 1906

Step Two:
Select what you would like to have, do, or be.

If you realize you can have anything, be anything, or do anything, then the question becomes: What do you want?

The trick is in turning every one of your complaints around to something you DO want. Start focusing on where you want to go, not on where you were or where you are.

I don't want this headache becomes "I want a clear head."

I don't want this back ache becomes "I want a strong back."

"I don't want these bills" becomes "I want more than enough money for everything I desire."

"I don't want to struggle in my business" becomes "I want business to come to me easily and effortlessly."

There's an art to rewriting what you don't want into what you do want. All I do is write the opposite of my complaint. Turn the sentence around 180 degrees. If I say, "I'm tired of being interrupted when I write," the opposite would be, "I want to write in a place that is safe, quiet and without interruptions."

You're probably wondering what this has to do with anything. Why write these sentences if they won't help you pay the bills or heal your problems or anything else?

Good question. The answer: Refocusing on what you do want will take you in the direction of what you want.

You see, we seem to create our lives out of our perceptions. If we focus on lack, we get more lack. If we focus on riches, we get more riches. Our perception becomes a magnet that pulls us in the direction of where we want to go.

If you don't consciously select where you want to go, you go where your unconscious wants you to go. To paraphrase the famous Swiss psychologist Carl Jung, "Until you make the unconscious conscious, it will direct your life and you will call it fate."

In that regard, most of us are on auto-pilot. We simply haven't realized that we can take the controls. Knowing what you want helps you aim your life in the direction you want to take it.

But there is a little more to it....

I just had lunch with a delightful friend of mine. She had a session with Jonathan last week and she was still glowing. Her eyes were large and alive, full of passion for life. She reminded me that even though you may think you know what you want, you may have to probe deeper to discover what you really want.

She had gone to see Jonathan with the intention of creating a successful business for herself. Jonathan asked, "For what purpose?" After dodging the question for a while, she realized that she wanted a successful business "to prove I am a worthwhile person."

I remember saying I wanted to write books that were colossal best sellers. Jonathan asked me that same famous question, "For what purpose?" At first I squirmed and said things like, "I deserve it" or "I want the money" or "My books are good enough for it." But the real reason, the underlying motivating factor, was that I wanted best selling books "so people would love and admire me." When I said it, I felt a shift within myself. I knew I had reached the real thing I wanted. My goal, my intention, was to feel love.

Most people live their entire lives being driven by an unconscious, unacknowledged need for something. The politician may be a child who never got enough attention. The business woman may be a youngster who doesn't feel equal to her peers. The best selling author may still be trying to prove he's smart, or lovable, or admirable.

Freedom and power come from knowing what you want without being a prisoner to what you want.

But there's another reason for knowing and stating your intention. When you declare it, you begin to discover all the things in the way of it happening. You may say you want to pay off your house so you are free of those big payments, but suddenly here come all of the objections: "I don't make enough money to pay off my house," or "No one ever does that!", to "What will my parents think?"

You know what I mean. It's easy to come up with objections. The trick is to dissolve those objections until you are clear inside. When you are, manifesting whatever you want will be easier.

Let me explain...

A woman went to see Jonathan because she was going to have a cancer operation on Monday. She saw him on Friday. She was terrified of the operation and wanted to get rid of her fears. Jonathan helped her release all of her fears, and two hours later, when she sat up on his table, she felt healed. But she still went through the operation. On Monday, when the Doctors opened her up, they could not find any cancer. It was gone.

What happened? Again, our beliefs are powerful. The woman believed she could remove the beliefs that were causing her fear, and she did. But she didn't know that the fear was what created the cancer. When she removed the fear, the cancer left. It no longer had a home in her body. She had taken conscious control of her life by choosing to see Jonathan and take care of her negative beliefs. She knew her life could be another way.

Beliefs are how we create reality. I'm not sure how to explain this to you in a way that makes sense. You've probably noticed that people seem to have recurring problems. Did you ever wonder why it was the same problem for each person? The person with money problems always has money problems. The person with relationship problems always has relationship problems. It's as though each person specializes in a disorder.

Beliefs, unconscious or not, are creating those events. Until the beliefs that create the events are released, the events will continue to reoccur. I know a man who has been married seven times. He hasn't gotten it right yet. He will continue to marry and divorce and marry until he removes the underlying beliefs that cause the events to happen. And while he continues to marry and divorce, he will blame other people for his problems, and maybe even blame fate, or God. But as you read earlier, "Until you make the unconscious conscious, it will direct your life and you will call it fate."

What are your beliefs?

Look at your life. What you have are the direct results of your beliefs. Not happy? In debt? Poor marriage? Not successful? Bad health? There are beliefs that are creating those experiences for you. In a very real sense, some part of you wants what you have---problems and all.

Joe Vitale

I remember motivational guru Tony Robbins talking about a schizophrenic woman who had diabetes when she was one personality and was healthy when she was another personality. Beliefs make up personality. The woman with diabetes had beliefs which created those diabetes. It's obvious that if you change the beliefs, you change the situation.

How do you change the beliefs? It starts with selecting what you want for your life. As soon as you select what you want to be, do, or have, you'll discover beliefs in the way of it. They'll surface. That swings back to what I was talking about earlier, that you can then restate your complaints so they become goals or intentions for you.

So, what do you want?

Use the space below to write want you want to be, do, or have. A study by Brian Tracy revealed that people who simply wrote down their wants and put the list away, discovered a year later that 80% of what they wrote came to be.

Write down your wants!

_____

_____

_____

_____

_____

_____

_____

_____

_____

_____

_____

_____

_____

_____

_____

_____

_____

_____

_____

_____

_____

Joe Vitale

Did you write down many goals?

Sometimes people feel greedy when they start to ask for what they want. They feel they are taking from others.

The best way around that limiting belief is to be sure you also want others to have success, too.

In other words, if you want a new house but don't want your neighbor to have one, you're stuck in ego and that's greed. But if you want a new house and think everyone ought to have one, then you are in tune with the creative spirit and you'll pull or be led to that new house.

You see, there really isn't any shortage in the world. The universe is bigger than our egos and can supply more then we can demand. Our job is to simply honestly ask for what we want. The desire in you is coming to you from your inner spirit. Honor that spirit by writing down what you really want to have, do or be:

_____

_____

_____

_____

_____

_____

_____

_____

_____

_____

_____

_____

_____

_____

_____

_____

_____

_____

_____

_____

_____

Now write down one goal or intention, something that you would really like to have, do, or be.

Focus brings power. Look over your two lists and see what goal or goals jump out at you. Which goal or intention has the most energy, or charge, on it? A goal should scare you a little and excite you a lot.

And keep in mind that you can always combine goals. There's nothing wrong with stating something like, "I want to weigh 120 pounds, own a brand new Corvette, and have fifty thousand dollars in the bank, by this coming Christmas."

In the space below, write down the most powerful intention you can:

_____

_____

_____

_____

_____

_____

Now here's the final step:

Write your intention as if you already have it.

In other words, "I want to weigh 120 pounds, own a brand new Corvette, and have fifty thousand dollars in the bank, by this coming Christmas" becomes "I now weigh 120 pounds, own a brand new Corvette, and have fifty thousand dollars in the bank!"

Do that now. Just rewrite your goal into present tense, pretending that you already have what you want:

_____

_____

_____

_____

_____

_____

_____

_____

You might now write the above goal on a card and put it in your pocket or purse. By doing so you will be unconsciously reminding yourself of your intention. Your own mind will then help nudge you in the direction of making your goal a reality.

So relax. You just planted a seed in your mind. The rest of this book will tell you how to water it, give it sunshine, clear out any weeds, and let it grow.

Prepare for your miracles!

Joe Vitale

"Prosperity is the ability to do what you want to do at the instant you want to do it."

-- *Treat Yourself to Life* by Raymond Charles Barker, 1954

Step Three:
Get clear.

Spot was a stray dog I claimed as my own when I was in college. But he used to run off and tear up the neighbor's gardens, run across the street and make drivers slam on their brakes, and just make a nuisance of himself. So I put him on a small leash. But I felt guilt for keeping this wonderful friend on a three foot leash. I bought a longer leash, six feet of freedom, and put it on Spot. I then walked six feet away and called Spot to me. He ran---three feet. He wouldn't go an inch beyond the length of the old leash. I had to walk over to Spot, put my arm around him, and walk him out the full six feet of new leash. From then on, he used all of that leash.

I think each of us has a limit we've placed on our freedom. We need a "miracles coach" to help us see that in reality we have no limits. Jonathan does that with his clients. But he does it in a way that may seem pretty strange to you. Hang on to your seat and let me see if I can explain it to you...

The first time I had a session with Jonathan I didn't know what to expect. I thought the man was a little strange because he couldn't articulate what he did. But I've been a curious journalist for many years, so I jumped in and did a session with him.

"What's your intention for this session?" Jonathan asked.

"What do you mean?"

"You can have anything you want. What do you want to focus on?"

I thought it over for a moment and then spoke.

"I want clarity on the book I am writing about Bruce Barton."

"What kind of clarity?"

"I want to know what I'm supposed to do next," I said.

"Okay. Let's go upstairs."

Jonathan had me lie down on his massage table. He gently guided me to breathe in different colors.

"Breathe the color red through the top of your head and imagine it going through your body and out of your feet."

We went through numerous colors.

"What other color do you need to breathe in?" he asked.

I said gray. He then asked me to breathe in that color. After several minutes of breathing deeply and relaxing on his massage table, Jonathan put his hand over my heart and said, "Open this up."

While I didn't consciously do anything, I felt a rush of electricity and energy shoot through me, almost blinding me. There was a strong white light surging through my body, blasting into my head, somehow illuminating the inside of my skull.

Suddenly I felt in the presence of angels, spirits, guides. I don't know how to explain it. But it was real. I felt it. I sensed it. I knew they were there. And these beings somehow worked on me, altering my beliefs, helping me realize I had more "leash" than I thought.

I'm not sure how long I was in that altered state. Twenty minutes? An hour? I don't know. When I finally sat up on the table, I noticed that Jonathan had a tear rolling down his cheek. When the energy started to blast through me, he moved aside to let it do its work. But the beauty and miracle of what he was seeing touched him. He was crying.

As my head cleared and I got my bearings, I realized I knew the next step for my book project. I was to go to

Joe Vitale

Wisconsin and continue my research by looking at the private papers of Bruce Barton at the historical museum. I had gotten my intention.

And that's not all.

Shortly after that first session with Jonathan I began to notice other changes in my outer life. The book I had been working on began to take direction. I found a publisher for it. I found the money to complete my research. I bought a new car. I bought a new house. My income soared.

How? Why?

I had invited the other side to help me, and it did.

As I write these words, I'm very aware that you may think I've lost my mind. After all, here I am, an adult, an author, a fairly well known speaker and marketing specialist who advises business executives about their work, talking about "spirits."

But I also know that you know what I mean. Even the most atheistic among us has been touched by the miraculous, the uncanny, or the unexplainable. While no one knows what awaits on the other side of this life, we all tend to believe something intelligent is there.

44

Maybe it's worth mentioning that the book that helped me the most here was *What Can A Man Believe?* by Bruce Barton. In it he explained that there was little proof for heaven after earth, but that it was far wiser to believe than not believe.

In other words, while I can't prove that angels and guides are standing ready to help you, isn't it a much more delicious and comforting and magical thought to believe in them then to not believe in them? There's no concrete evidence to support them or deny them. But when you can use the belief in them to create miracles, wouldn't you be wise to do so?

Yesterday a friend of mine called and said she wanted to believe in guides and angels and teachers from the spiritual side of life, but a part of her doubted they existed.

"That's okay," I said. "I have my doubts, as well."

"You do?"

"Sure," I said. "If I had to go into a court of law and prove I had spirit guides, they would laugh me out of the courthouse. There's no proof for them, but also there's no proof against them."

And then I remembered something I had read in a recent issue of Reader's Digest, where Larry Dossey talked about prayer. He said praying helped people recover from illness. In many cases they recovered from what Doctors had said were "incurable" illnesses. What these successful patients did was pray. Even the patients admitted they didn't know if the prayers were answered, but it was the belief in the praying and the act of praying that helped them anyway. Again, as Barton pointed out, it is wiser to believe than not to believe. Believing helps create miracles.

Barton wrote this passage in 1927, in his book *What Can A Man Believe*? I've always loved it as it seems to stir the very something he talks about within me. See what it does for you:

"In every human being, whether emperor or cowboy, prince or pauper, philosopher or slave, there is a mysterious something which he neither understands nor controls. It may lie dormant for so long as to be almost forgotten; it may be so repressed that the man supposes it is dead. But one night he is alone in the desert under the starry sky; one day he stands with bowed head and damp eyes beside an open grave; or there comes an hour when he clings with desperate instinct to the wet rail of a storm-tossed boat, and suddenly out of the forgotten depths of his being this mysterious something leaps forth. It over-reaches habit; it pushes aside reason, and with a voice that will not be denied it cries out its questionings and its prayer."

So let's assume you don't have access to Jonathan (though you can reach me, and other healers and mentors by emailing the people in the back of this book). What can you do?

Easy. Focus on what you want, and make one of your intentions finding someone to help you clear yourself of old beliefs so you can create the life you want. Help exists. State your intention to the world and allow it to come to you.

I feel it's important to have support from a mentor. It's too easy to fall back into the old way of thinking, to feel sorry for ourselves and play the role of victim. The vast majority of your current friends probably won't support your desire to create miracles. When I first started seeing Jonathan, I would visit him once a month. He and I quickly saw that we needed to stay in touch at least once a week. Me and Jonathan made a pact that said, "Whenever I'm not clear, I am to call him." Then, whenever I let something in life throw me for a tailspin, I would call him.

Another woman recently asked me what it meant to "get clear" with my beliefs. I thought about it for a while before I could answer. The image that came to me was of a football team. If one of those players is hurting, upset, feeling neglected, angry because the coach overlooked him earlier or his girlfriend dumped him, that one player can jeopardize or sabotage the entire team's success.

You are like the whole football team. If all parts of you, all of the beliefs inside of you, are in alignment, no problem. You'll achieve your desires. But if any part of you, any belief in you, doesn't support your intention, it will jeopardize or sabotage you. That's why you may have had lousy luck at love, romance, money or health. Some part of you doesn't want it. We need to heal that part. When you do, you are clear.

How do you know if you are clear right now?
Think of something that you want to have, do, or be.

Why don't you have it yet?

If your answer is something negative, you aren't clear. If you say anything except an honest "I know it's on the way to me," you probably aren't clear inside with what you want.

Another question to ask yourself is, "What does it mean that you don't yet have what you want?"

Your answer to that question will reveal your beliefs. For example, if you say, "I have to do such and such first," then you have a belief that you have to do something before you can have what you want.

If you say, "My soul doesn't want me to have this," then you are stating your own beliefs about what you think your soul wants for you.

If you say, "I don't know how to get what I want," then you are revealing a belief that says you have to know how to get what you want before you can have it.

Your beliefs aren't that hard to find.

Self-help author Mandy Evans says certain beliefs can lead to a very bad day. Beliefs cause stress, not your business or life situations.

"There's what happened to you in your life and then there's what you decided it meant," says Evans, author of *Travelling Free: How to Recover from the Past by Changing Your Beliefs.*

"Change your conclusions, or your beliefs about the events in your past," explains Evans, "and you can change the way you live your life today. Certain beliefs can really trip us up."

Beliefs shape the way we feel, think and act, says Evans, an expert in personal belief systems. But you can't change them until you know what they are. Evans offers a list of "The Top 20 Self-Defeating Beliefs" in *Travelling Free*, her second book, as a way to begin exploring them.

"As you look at each belief, ask yourself if you believe it," suggests Evans. "If you do, then ask yourself why you believe it. Gently explore your own reasons for buying into any self-limiting belief."

Here are ten of her Top 20 limiting beliefs.

1. I'm not good enough to be loved.
2. No matter what I do, I should be doing something else.
3. If it hasn't happened yet, it never will.

4. If you know what I'm really like, you wouldn't want me.

5. I don't know what I want.

6. I upset people.

7. Sex is dirty and nasty; save it for the one you love.

8. Better stop wanting; if you get your hopes up, you'll get hurt.

9. If I fail, I should feel bad for a long time and be really scared to try again.

10. I should have worked this out by now.

Those are all beliefs. Sometimes you need another person to point out your beliefs. When my friend Linda and I had breakfast one day, and I hired her to help me with some promotion, she said, "I'm afraid some of my friends will be jealous of me."

"That's a belief," I said.

Linda's eyes widened and her face lit up.

"It is?" she asked.

It had never occurred to her that her fear was a belief--a belief she could let go of. She needed another person to shine a light on the belief.

Here's another example of what I mean:

I'm now driving the fourth new car of my dreams thanks to Jonathan's magic in helping me get clear with my desire.

I needed a car bad. The one I was driving was an old clunker that could only move if you pushed it. Okay, it wasn't that bad. But whenever the car broke down, I broke down. Paying the repair bills was killing me. And never knowing if the car would get me where I was going was stressing me out. I needed help. I called Jonathan because of my fear of car salespeople (I had been one once and knew of their tactics). I told Jonathan what I wanted.

He said, "What you really want is often under what you say you want....What would having this new car do for you?"

Huh?

Jonathan went on to explain that what we want may be a feeling rather than a product. Focus on the feeling and it will help me get what I really want. What would I feel if I had a new car?

What a mind stopper! I developed a brain squeezing headache just thinking about it. I got off the phone and my head began to throb as if it had been hit with a sledge hammer. Though I almost never take medicine, I ate a handful of aspirin like it was popcorn. It didn't help.

I went to see Jonathan in person. Sitting in the presence of his accepting energy, letting my pain "speak" to me, I suddenly saw the ache between my eyes as a huge black ball of tightly woven thread. Mentally a thread would loosen and I'd hear a belief:

"You can't afford a new car."

I let it go and another belief would unravel:

"What would your Dad say about this car?"

And then another thread/belief would slide out:

"How will you afford it?"

And then another....and another...and another....

As these beliefs slowly came apart and left, the black ball of pain got smaller. And smaller. Within twenty minutes, the headache was completely gone! I was healed. I was clear. I was happy.

Now get this:

Though I didn't think it was really possible, I followed my intuition and immediately went to the car dealership I felt led to visit. Consciously I "knew" there was no way I could get a new car. (I had never had a NEW car in my entire life and my credit was lousy). But I let go. I trusted.

I went to the car dealership and the gentleman there let me look around. I told him what I wanted and he said he had one car that fit the description. We walked out back and he was right. It was perfect. It was gold and beautiful and new. I said, "Does it have a cassette player?" He looked and nodded. "Well," I said, "let's do the hard part. Let's see if I can buy it."

We filled out forms and he asked me to place a deposit. I didn't. I wasn't confident enough to think I would get the car, so I put nothing down on it. I then left. I drove to a friend's outside of the city and we played music all day, he strumming his guitar and me blowing on my harmonica. Later in the afternoon I decided to call the dealership.

"You qualify," said the salesperson.

I was stunned.

"I do? Are you looking at my paperwork?" I asked. "I'm Joe Vitale."

He laughed and assured me he was. He then asked me when I wanted to pick up my car. I went and picked up the car, in delighted shock that it was mine. While I had no idea how I would make the payments, I did. It's now been four years and I'm on my fourth new car. I've never been late for a payment. In fact, I mail my checks in early.

And that's not all.

As soon as I decided to get the new car, my life went into an upward spiral of magical coincidences.

Suddenly the money I needed appeared. Clients began to call. Classes sold out. I was invited to speak to groups I had never heard of. And two publishers gave me book offers on the very same day.

In some real way, my allowing the car in my life sent a message to the universe that I was TRUSTING. Instead of worrying and wondering how I'd pay the bills, I leaped off the mountain top of fear and---to my surprise---I didn't fall.

I soared.

But I had to get clear inside before any of this could happen. Had I gone to buy a new car when I was still carrying limiting beliefs about what I could have afforded, my beliefs would have sabotaged my purchase. I would have created not paying for the car to support the beliefs. The first thing that had to happen was clearing the beliefs.

Lynda Madden Dahl, in her book *Beyond the Winning Streak*, lists several limiting beliefs concerning money. Here are a few of them:

* "I must work hard for the money I earn."
* "I need more money than I can generate."
* "I feel helpless in changing my financial picture."

What you want to do is replace negative beliefs with positive ones, such as:

* "Money is a natural manifestation of the universe."
* "It's OK to be rich."
* "I don't have to work hard for my money."
* "I am destined for great wealth."

You see, the beliefs you have were given to you when you were a child. You simply absorbed them. Now you are becoming awakened. You are at choice. You can choose to let go of the beliefs you don't want, and you can choose to replace the beliefs with ones that better serve you.

Isn't that a wonderful feeling---to know that you can now create your life the way you want it to be?

Clearing beliefs can be an easy process. The easiest time I ever had was when I wanted to overcome my sinus allergies.

I had suffered terrible sinus infections and sinus headaches for years. I can't begin to describe how miserable they made me feel. I took herbs. I had acupuncture treatments. I wore air purifiers. Everything helped but nothing worked permanently.

Then one day I asked my dear friend Mrs. Kathy DeMont, a Remote Healer, if she would try to help me. We were having dinner and I looked her in the eye, slammed my fist on the table, and said, "I don't want relief. I want healed. I want this thing gone."

My intensity shook her. But she also realized how sincere I was and how much pain I had been in. She said she would try to help.

And she did. She went home, got quiet, and used her skills to clear my body. I was not present as she did this. I wasn't even aware that she did anything. But within a few days I noticed that I could breathe again. I called her and asked what she had done.

"You had some negative energy in you and I scared it off," she said.

Apparently, she was able to use her remote healing skills to clear my beliefs and my energy from a distance.

Talk about making things easy for me!

Here's another example of clearing beliefs. This one still amazes me, because it happened to my wife and I saw the dramatic change.

Marian never learned to drive a car. I was her chauffeur for more than 15 years. I'm not complaining. That's just the way it was.

But after seeing my changes with my work with Jonathan and other healers, Marian wondered if she could get clear about driving. She booked a session with Jonathan. Within one hour she was clear.

What happened? Marian remembered being a little girl and being in the back seat of her Mom's car as her Mom learned how to drive. Her Mom was naturally nervous.

Marian picked up on that energy and locked onto it. While Marian went on to grow up, the little girl who sat in the back seat of her Mom's car remained alive in her. As an adult, that little girl kept Marian from driving.

Under Jonathan guidance, Marian was able to remember that experience and release it. She realized it was an old memory and it no longer served her. She let it go. Her energy was now clear.

And today Marian drives her own car---a new one, to boot---and she loves it. I remember one night there was a terrible storm in Houston with lots of flooding. I was worried about my wife and how she would handle the weather. When she got home late that night, I ran to the garage to greet her.

What I saw amazed me. Marian was smiling ear to ear. Her face was beaming. She rolled down her window and said, "I had an adventure!"

Even being stuck in traffic is something Marian now feels grateful for. She simply sits there and listens to music.

And one day we went to lunch in separate cars. After it, I was behind her at a stop light. I saw her moving her lips and tapping her fingers on the steering wheel. I wondered if she were getting impatient. Then I pulled up closer and realized she was singing and taping her fingers to the music!

Talk about a transformation!

During the writing of this book, Marian was in a bad car accident. She was hit by a van, and hit hard enough to break the back axle on her car. Despite the shock of it all, Marian was fine, though her car wasn't.

Now here's the juicy part: Two days later Marian was ready to rent a car and start driving again. I couldn't believe it. I told her I was proud of her, that many people are too nervous to drive so soon after an accident.

Marian just looked at me, smiled, and said, "Why? Driving is too much fun not to do it!"

Jonathan has a saying, "It's all energy." What he means is that we are energy systems. If we are clear, the energy moves in one direction. If we aren't clear, the energy moves in several directions, and without full power.

Caroline Myss, a medical intuitive and author of *Anatomy of the Spirit*, talks about being "plugged into" the past. If there was a situation in your life where you were hurt, abused, or anything unfinished, you are probably still carrying around that unfinished business. You are still plugged into that old event. That means a part of your energy is still back there, reliving and probably recreating the old event.

I know this is tough to understand. But let's use another example from Myss. Think of the energy you get each day as cash. You wake up in the morning with $500 available for the day. But you are still mad because your spouse said something mean to you last night. That's going to cost you. You are spending $50 to keep that energy alive in you.

And say you are still upset because a friend owes you money from five years ago. Now you are spending $100 to keep that memory alive.

And let's assume you were abused as a child. You are spending another $100 to keep that memory in you. You woke up with $500 to spend but before you get out of bed you have spent half of it on old memories.

When you try to manifest something today, you won't have all of your energy available to make it happen. When you get clear of the old events, hurts, memories and beliefs, you will have more energy to create what you want now. And the more energy you have now, the more you will get.

You will end up like the supermodel who once said, "I don't wake up for less than $10,000 a day."

Another saying Jonathan has is "The energy you give out is the results you get."

Yes, he's great at coming up with mind benders like that. But I think he means that the beliefs you have create the results you get. If you are unconsciously sending out vibes that attract lousy conditions, you will experience lousy conditions.

One of my clients wrote a book about children who had been molested. He pointed out that the criminal could always easily pick the person who he was going to molest. That child always sent out vibes that said "woe is me" or "I'm a victim." Though we aren't wearing signs on our backs or on our foreheads, somehow the energy we walk around with creates the situations we get. "The energy you give out is the results you get."

If you find yourself recreating similar events---like my friend who has been married seven times so far---you know you are stuck in an energy pattern that will continue to create those events until it gets dissolved.

My dear friend Karol Truman, author of the great book *Feelings Buried Alive Never Die*, put it this way:

"It's the continual suppression of unresolved feelings and emotions that cause the problems we experience in our lives."

I can hear you now: "How can I get out of this pattern?"

One of the fundamental principles of Jonathan Jacobs' work is that everything is energy. It's not a new idea. Stuart Wilde writes about it in his books. Joseph Murphy refers to it in his works. Bob Proctor talks about it in his seminars. Scientists are discovering it, as well. Nothing exists but energy formed into things we then name, like tables, chairs, houses, cars, people.

The thing is, you and I are different from tables, chairs, houses, and cars because we are spiritual. That's the miracle of our lives!

As Bob Proctor once told me, "Although everything is energy, the difference between people and objects is that we are spiritual. That means we have the means to alter and influence other energies. We can change the energy of a table, chair, house, car, or even other people."

Taken a step further, it means we are all connected. If we're nothing but energy and we're all one, then what you do affects me and what I do affects you, even if we're miles or even continents apart.

Got it?

Oh.

Well, neither did I, at first.

So let's look at a couple of stories that may help.

One day a client of mine hired me to be his marketing wizard. He gave me a lot of money and I hired some folks to help me. All went well. Months passed. Then one day the bomb dropped.

My client suddenly sent me a letter saying I had lied to him. It was two pages of pain for me to read. It got pretty confusing and it made me dizzy, confused, and shocked. I had meetings with my staff and I even called my client. I couldn't figure out why this was happening. I sent the client a two page letter explaining my position. Next day I got another two page letter from him, almost as shocking. Finally I went to Jonathan.

"The key word is trust," Jonathan pointed out. "You keep saying he didn't trust you. Let's look at how that applies to you. Where in your own life aren't you trusting?"

This is typical of Jonathan. He'll have you look at your own life to see how what you are complaining about is relevant. In a way, you use your experiences as mirrors. You use the outer to see what you are doing inside. (Stay with me on this.)

I thought and said, "Well, I've never done marketing like this before. He's hired me to direct his entire marketing campaign and expects me to lead his staff to victory. I guess I don't trust that I can do it."

"And that's what your client is picking up on an energy level. That's the signal you are sending out."

"What do we do?"

"Are you willing to release the fear and feel the trust?"

"Yes."

And that's about all it took. I felt a shift inside me and I felt like I knew I could trust myself to do the job. I let go and breathed a sigh of relief. I feel it happened so easily

65

Joe Vitale

because most of me was already clear with the problem. I didn't have a lot of work to do in clearing old beliefs.

Now here comes the good part.

I went home and called my client. He answered and sounded remarkably at peace. I told him I was going to do a great job for him.

"I know you are," he said, stunning me. "I decided a little while ago to just trust the man I hired to do his job."

"You decided a little while ago? When?"

Yes, he had decided to trust me about the time Jonathan and I looked at the trust issue in me. Once it was clear in me, my client felt it. Once I sent out a different signal, my client picked it up.

Coincidence? Then let me tell you another story...

Another client of mine went on to great fame and fortune. He's a 25 year old stockbroker who wrote a book on wealth. I knew it would be a success before he did. I acted as his literary agent and marketing consultant and went to work to find a publisher for his book. As it worked out, he left me and went to an agent in Dallas, thereby cutting me out of the $45,000 in profits I would have earned from his $300,000 advance. But he's a very honorable guy and said he would pay me some money when he got his big advance.

Days passed.

Weeks passed.

Months passed.

Nothing.

I wrote him a few kind notes. I sent him copies of my articles to share my own successes. I called him a few times and left messages.

Still nothing.

I asked Jonathan about it. He suggested I write a letter to the client and state my feelings, state what I want, and forgive him. I went home and did that. It felt very good.

But still nothing.

I went to Jonathan and said I did what he told me but still no reply.

"What does that mean?" he asked.

"It means he hasn't contacted me yet."

"And?"

"And it means he may rip me off."

"There it is," Jonathan announced.

"Where what is?" I asked.

"It's the fear of being ripped off that is blocking your energy. That's the belief in your way."

"How do I let go of that?"

"Feel that feeling of being ripped off."

I closed my eyes and did so.

"Let it take you back to the other times when you may have been in experiences where you decided on beliefs about money and people."

I recalled being taken by a Dallas company for money I had nearly died to earn. I had felt cheated. I held a grudge against that company for nearly eight years. I breathed into that feeling and felt a shift inside. I opened my eyes and smiled.

"The money he owes you doesn't have to come from him," Jonathan explained. "The universe is prosperous and can give you money in a wide variety of ways. Release the need for him to pay you and you allow the money to come."

Accepting that concept is a biggie. It means totally letting go of any and all grudges against people. It means trusting that you will get what you want, as long as you aren't attached to how it comes to you.

I felt like the release was there. I felt lighter and clearer.

And when I got home there was a message from-- my client!

After six months of nothing, suddenly a call! He was very polite, very friendly, and said he was mailing me a four-figure check. He did, too, as I received it the next day. I feel only a fool would call that experience a coincidence. The connection is too obvious, and happens to me too often, to blow over as mere chance.

As Jonathan says, it's all energy and we're all connected. Clean the energy pathways and you can have, do, or be anything you want.

If you feel that you have cleaned your energy circuits and are free from the past and yet you aren't making money or miracles or anything else, then you haven't cleaned your energy circuits or gotten free from the past.

This happened to me a few years ago. After doing several sessions with Jonathan by phone, I realized that my income wasn't increasing. My bills were being paid and money was arriving just in the nick of time to pay them, but it was too close for my comfort. I began to get worried. Not a good sign. My worry was evidence that I had some unfinished business to clear up. I wanted to contact Jonathan, but he was not available.

Then one day Bill Ferguson offered to give me one of his sessions. Bill is a former divorce attorney who has created a way to help people release the key core issue that sabotages their lives. He's been on Oprah, and he's written several books, including *Heal the Hurt that Runs Your Life*. I was helping Bill with his publicity and he wanted me to experience what he does. When he said I could have a session with him, I accepted. Especially since it was free. Now that I have had it, I would have been willing to pay anything for it.

"People are starving to learn how to find peace," Bill told me when I went to his Houston suite. "But they keep looking outside of themselves and blaming people or circumstances for how they feel. That's not how life works."

He asked me to think about a recent event that pushed my button. That was a snap. I had just fired a client of mine who didn't agree with my ideas on how to promote his business. I was insulted and angry.

"Note that how you felt had nothing to do with the other person. All the person did was reactivate your hurt by pushing the right button. Once you disconnect the hurt, your hot button for emotional pain won't be there.

"Every one of us has a hurt from the past that runs our life," Bill added. "For one person, the hurt is failure. For another, it's the hurt of feeling worthless, not good enough, not worth loving, or some other form of not feeling okay with who they are."

He added that avoiding these feelings creates emotional pain.

"Until a person releases the core issue, it will continue to operate," Bill told me. "You could be ninety years old and still recreating painful experiences because of a core belief you accepted when you were six."

While many psychotherapies believe people have unresolved past issues, few claim they can be healed quickly. Bill developed a new technology that helps people release their emotional pain---and in under two hours. You might say he has created a way to achieve "push button healing."

"Pick another event where you were upset," Bill told me.

I did. Again, it was easy. While I hadn't thought about it before, I suddenly began to see a pattern. Almost every time I was upset with someone, it was because I felt insulted.

"What does it mean that you feel insulted?" Bill probed.

After a moment, I realized it meant that I didn't feel good enough. I must not be good enough, went my logic, because these people don't like what I am doing and I end up being insulted.

Now Bill started to rub my nose in it.

"How's it feel to not be good enough?" he asked.

I was getting depressed. I looked into Bill's boyish face, wondering if he really wanted me to feel this bad. He did.

"Until you can fully feel the hurt that's been buried alive inside you, it will continue to operate and sabotage your life."

Whew. By now I was feeling like life itself wasn't worth living.

"If you are truly feeling the key issue for you, you should be feeling like life isn't worth living."

"I'm there, Bill. I'm there," I said, slowly.

"Good!" Bill declared. "So how's it feel to be not good enough?"

"Like the worst feeling I've ever felt."

"Can you accept that you really aren't good enough?"

I struggled with that one. While I could look at my life and clearly find evidence that I was good enough, I had to admit that I wasn't good enough in all areas. And I had to further admit that this belief that I "wasn't good enough" was unconsciously causing me to be upset with clients and friends. I had been losing many opportunities. Even money.

"Yes, I can admit it."

Something shifted right there. I somehow felt lighter. More relaxed. Free. Where before I felt tense and angry, now I felt relaxed and calm. Even happy. It was as if some giant electrical wiring had been disconnected and I suddenly looked at life differently.

Joe Vitale

Bill and I did some additional work before I left. But after the session, I noticed major differences. Nothing seemed to irritate me like it used to. The next day I had a client argue about an ad I wrote for him and this time I didn't fly off the handle. I calmly stated my case. And I noticed that I looked at each moment with love and optimism. And I saw that I wasn't afraid to do things that I used to not do at all, like play the guitar in front of friends. Before I didn't feel good enough. And I also noticed that money started to roll in. One morning a few days after my work with Bill a woman faxed me that she was sending me a check for several thousand dollars to begin promoting her business.

What had happened? Now that the core belief was disconnected, I had opened the energy centers in me to allow the abundance of the universe to flow my way.

And flow it did.

In Wayne Dyer's book, *Manifest Your Destiny*, he says if you aren't manifesting what you want, there probably is an absence of love somewhere in your inner world.

That's another way of discovering where you may not be clear inside. Think of how you feel about the people involved in what you want to create. If there is a negative "charge" or uncomfortable feeling about someone, you aren't clear with that person.

Forgiveness is the best way I know for getting clear by yourself. And the best way to become forgiving is to feel gratitude. I'll talk more about gratitude a little later, but for now know that if you focus on what you like about people, you will feel grateful, and then you will begin to forgive, and then you will get clear.

And when you get clear, you can have, do, or be whatever you want.

Here's one more easy way for you to get clear, and it's something you can do on your own. I learned it from my friend Bob Proctor, at one of his famous Science of Getting Rich seminars...

Take two sheets of paper.

On the first sheet describe the negative condition you are in. Describe the picture of the situation as it is now, and really feel the emotions associated with it. This probably won't feel great. But you want to get into that feeling, because the more you feel it, the more you will release it. In other words, whatever emotion you suppress will sooner or later need to be expressed. While it's suppressed, it's clogging up your inner vibration. Release it and you free your energy to go out and manifest what you want. Let your feelings come to the surface as you describe this situation or condition that you don't want.

Now put that first sheet aside.

Take the second sheet and begin to write out how you want the situation or condition to be. Get into the joyful feeling associated with having or doing or being the thing you desire. Really immerse yourself in this good energy. Describe the situation the way you want it to be, and paint this wonderful picture so completely that you can feel it as you write it. Just as you wanted to experience the negative emotion so you could release it, you now want to experience the positive emotion so you can create a new picture to anchor in your subconscious. The more you can fall in love with this new image and these new feelings, the faster you will manifest them.

Now take the first sheet, look it over, and burn it.

Take the second sheet, fold it up, and carry it with you for a week.

You're done. You probably just cleared yourself of your negative block. And if it should ever resurface, just do the exercise again.

See! It's easy!

Finally, let me give you one more method for clearing yourself. This one doesn't cost any money, doesn't take more than a minute to do, doesn't hurt at all, and is guaranteed to work every time.

Interested?

The method involves a simple script that you say out loud to release a belief or a feeling you no longer want, and to replace it with something you prefer. I learned it from my friend Karol Truman, author of the truly amazing book, *Feelings Buried Alive Never Die....*

I'll give you the Script in a moment. First, understand that this powerful tool is so simple, it's easy to dismiss. All you're asked to do is say a couple paragraphs of words. That's it!

Joe Vitale

Yet what the Script does is reprogram your basic DNA structure. It speaks to your spirit and asks it to help you get clear on the most fundamental levels of your being.

I don't want to complicate things here by trying to explain how this process works. My job is to give you the tools and show you how to use them. After all, you don't need to know how a FAX machine works in order to send or receive a FAX. All you do is insert the paper and it does the rest.

The Script is the same way. All you do is say it, inserting in the appropriate place what you are feeling at the time that you want to clear, and inserting in the appropriate place what you prefer to feel. This will make more sense once you know the words in the Script, so here they are:

Spirit, please locate the origin of my feeling/thought of feeling negative about (Insert the feeling or belief you want to release here) _____.

Take each and every level, layer, area and aspect of my be-ing to this origin. Analyze and resolve it perfectly, with God's truth.

Come forward in time, healing every incident based upon the foundation of the first, according to God's will; until I'm at the present, filled with light and truth, God's peace and love, forgiveness of myself for my incorrect perceptions, forgiveness of every person, place, circumstance and event which contributed to this feeling/thought.

With total forgiveness and unconditional love I delete the old from my DNA, release it, and let it go now! I feel (Insert the way you want to feel here) _____!! I allow every physical, mental, emotional and spiritual problem, and inappropriate behavior based on the old feelings to quickly disappear.

Thank you, Spirit, for coming to my aid and helping me attain the full measure of my creation. Thank you, thank you, thank you! I love you and praise God from whom all blessings flow.

Simple, isn't it?

Now, if you don't believe the Script will work for you, use the Script on that belief.

In other words, insert "Help me release my doubt about the power of this Script," in the first open spot in the Script. That's where you insert the belief or feeling you desire releasing.

In the second spot in the Script, insert the belief you prefer, which might be, "I now understand that any belief can be changed in just a moment, even with such a simple tool as this Script."

Again, this Script is powerful. Read Karol's wonderful book for a detailed explanation of it. Meanwhile, use the Script whenever you feel the need to get clear.

It works--almost like magic!

And once you are clear, you can truly have anything you can imagine!

Isn't this a fun, exciting, even exhilerating way to live?

"We learn the lessons in life we are to learn two ways: either through obedience to natural laws or through suffering the consequences of not observing those laws...None of us consciously create the suffering we experience."

-- Karol Truman, *Feelings Buried Alive Never Die...*, 1998

Step Four:
Feel how exciting it would be to have, do, or be what you want.

Marketing specialists know that people don't act for logical reasons, but for emotional ones. Emotion has power. Emotion also has the power to create what you want. Find within yourself what it will feel like to have, be, or do the thing you want and you will begin to manifest the thing you want. The energy in the emotion will work to pull you toward the thing you want while also pulling the thing you want toward you.

I know, I know. I'm getting philosophical again. But I'm writing about spiritual concepts, which few people can relate to. It's easy to see why. We are taught from the crib to pay attention to reality, to obey the laws of man, to worship books and leaders. While that can help our society run smoother (actually, it hasn't worked, but that's another book), it limits you. Belief in leaders, rules, and outside authorities limits you from creating the life you want. I once told a friend that a belief in a guru can limit her own power to manifest what she wanted. When you give your power away to anyone, you are spending your own energy in their direction.

One of the most powerful energies you can ever experience is gratitude. Feel gratefulness for anything and you shift the way you feel. Feel thankful for your life, your lungs, your home, this book; it doesn't matter. Once you feel grateful, you are in an energy that can create miracles.

Jonathan taught me this. I remember going to see him when I was broke and depressed. One of the first things he did was guide me into realizing that I had plenty in my life. When you compare your own life to that of people living in third world countries, you quickly see that you are living like a King or Queen. You probably have food, water, and shelter, as well as a refrigerator, a television, a radio, and probably a computer. Millions of people don't. Realize you are blessed with enormous abundance right now, feel grateful for it, and you will attract even more abundance.

My friend Jonathan Morningstar once cured himself of a terrible illness with a simple one line statement of gratitude.

Jonathan got double pneumonia. Nothing seemed to help him. Then he felt inspired to write down one simple but potent sentence that he repeated every hour, recorded on audiotape and played back to himself, and wrote on signs which he hung around his home. He made this one liner part of his very being.

And within twenty-four hours, Jonathan was healed.

What was the one line he used?

"Thank you God for all the blessings I have and for all the blessings I am receiving."

I'm not a scientist so I won't pretend to explain how this works. Somehow your energy sends off signals that attract more of what you are sending off. Like the child who unconsciously says he's a victim, you send off signals that attract what you are getting. Change your signals and you will change your results. Change your energy and you will change what you experience. "The energy you give out is the results you get."

Again, gratitude can shift everything. Just start feeling sincerely grateful for what you have. Look at your hands, or this book, or your pet, anything you feel love and gratitude for. Dwell on that feeling.

That's the energy that can help you manifest whatever you want.

Another energy you want to experience is the energy that comes from imagining what it will feel like to have, be, or do the thing you want. This can be fun.

Imagine how good it will be to have what you want, to be what you are wanting, to do what you dream. Feel the electrifying feelings that come with the images. These feelings can create the life you want. They can manifest it for you. Somehow those feelings lead you, guide you, direct you to do the things that will make the events.

The great German thinker Goethe may have said it best when he wrote the following inspiring message:

> *Until one is committed,*
> *there is hesitancy,*
> *the chance to draw back,*
> *always ineffectiveness.*
>
> *Concerning all acts of initiative*
> *there is one elementary truth,*

the ignorance of which kills
countless ideas and endless plans:
That the moment one definitely commits oneself,
then providence moves, too.

All sorts of things occur to help one
that would never otherwise have occurred.
A whole stream of events issues from the decision,
raising in one's favor all manner of
unforeseen incidents and meetings and
material assistance which no man
could have dreamed would come his way.

Whatever you can do or
dream you can, begin it!
Boldness has genius, power,
and magic in it.

I was in Seattle once to see friends. One night I turned on the television and caught the ending of a fascinating Larry King interview with the famous actor and singer, Andy Griffith. Andy was talking about one of his first motion pictures. He said something unknowingly metaphysical when he talked about a director who told him:

"The camera is just a machine. It picks up what you give it. All you have to do is think something, and feel it, and the camera will record it."

They then cut to a scene from the movie Griffith was referring to, when he was to look at a woman with a heart full of lust. You could tell from the actor's eyes that he was projecting thoughts that were pretty hot. Larry King later said, "It was one of the most X-rated looks in movie history."

The universe is like the movie camera. Think something and feel something and the universe will pick it up and project it. The advice Andy Griffith was given as a young actor is advice I want to give to us: When you know what you want, all you really have to do is think it and feel it. That's it. The universe---the spirit of all that exists---will pick up your signal and project it.

This is powerful stuff. When Jonathan and I practiced this, our energy levels shot skyward. We had so much energy surging through us that the very electrical outlets in our homes burst into flames. This is the truth! When I lived in the dump I could barely afford to pay rent for, the electrical system there fried. It cost the landlord over $7,000 to repair it.

When Jonathan was first experimenting with energy, the fuse box in his garage caught on fire. While this isn't why they call me "Mr. Fire!", it does demonstrate that when you make changes internally, you'll see changes externally. Jonathan had to have a new fuse box put in. My landlord replaced the entire electrical system in the house. But as my energy increased, I also had to move into a bigger home with better wiring.

Again, what you embrace in your inner world creates what you experience in your outer reality.

Jonathan and I were having lunch at a favorite Chinese restaurant one day when I noticed there was hardly anyone in the place. The owners looked worried. They were huddled around their cash register and talking. Usually they come over to us, smile, talk, and treat us like royalty. It was clear something was wrong. I mentioned this to Jonathan, saying, "They seem concerned about money."

Jonathan replied, "That's why they're concerned."

At first my mind screeched to a halt. But then I started laughing. Jonathan asked me what was so funny. I explained as best I could:

"Were you a Zen master in a past life or something?" I began. "What you just said was one of those unanswerable mind stretchers that Zen masters come up with."

"What do you mean?"

"I said those people look worried about money and you said that's why they're worried about money. To the outside world, that makes no sense."

"But it's the truth," Jonathan explained. "Their concern for money was something already in them that got manifested. Now they notice it in the outer world. They manifested their belief."

He then went on to tell me about a man he had worked with who ran an Indian restaurant and was failing at it. Business was lousy. He did a session with Jonathan and realized he didn't want to run a restaurant at all. Once he was clear, he let go of the restaurant and sold it. As a result, people started going to it under its new owner.

"Once you take care of the inner, it will show results in the outer," says Jonathan.

Another time he told me, "When you get the lessons, you don't need the experiences."

As bizarre as all of that dialogue might seem to you, it's been the truth in my experience as well.

One time a company hired me to help promote one of their Dallas seminars. I advised them on what to do and then I got angry when I saw that they did the opposite. They were, in essence, screwing up their own success.

I talked to Jonathan about it. He asked me what I got out of this. In other words, what was the benefit to me? Assuming a part of me did create the company doing everything wrong, how would it serve me? I thought about it and had the answer.

"Their screw-up takes the pressure to succeed off of me," I said. "They hired me to help them make the seminar a success. I wasn't sure I could do it. By their not listening to me, they have almost guaranteed that the seminar will fail. When it does, I can point my fingers at THEM and say, 'You did it, not me.'"

It keeps coming back to what we are doing and feeling inside plays a giant hand in what we end up experiencing.

No matter what the situation you are in, some part of you helped create it.

Get in touch with it, release the old beliefs and energy, and you can move toward creating what would serve you better and bring you more joy. One of the best ways to do just that is to focus on what you want, on how it would feel to have it, be it, do it.

One wonderful technique to help you in this area is called scripting.

I first heard of this method from Jerry and Esther Hicks. The concept is deceptively simple:

Just imagine that you already have what you want and write out a scene that describes it. Describe in such detail that you can feel it. Pretend you are a movie director and write a script for what you want to experience. Really get into it as you write it. Feel it. Sense it. Experience it.

I have a notebook full of scripts. Every one I have written has come into reality. Again, when you think it and feel it, it comes to be.

It's worth mentioning right here that your business cards, letterhead, flyers, sales letters, and ads---everything you produce or hire someone to produce to market your business---all carry your energy in them.

Think back to some flyer or letter you received in your mail. As soon as you glanced at it, you felt one way or another about the service. You may have had an instant feeling that said "This looks interesting" or an instant one that told you "Trash this."

I'm not just talking about the look of the marketing piece, though that is part of it. When you or anyone you hire creates a marketing document, they put their thoughts and feelings into what they create. People don't have to be psychic to pick up on this vibe. If you unconsciously don't believe in your product or service, that belief will appear in your marketing materials. And people will sense it. And you won't get business.

Again, feeling brings on miracles. When you know what you want, are clear about having it, and can feel the energy of what you want, you will begin to pull it to you. And when you clearly feel this energy, you will create marketing pieces that convey it. Here's an example of what I mean:

When I wrote a sales letter for a software product that I totally believed in, I got staggering results. People read the letter and sensed my sincerity and the product's benefits. As a result, over six percent of them sent in checks. In the world of direct mail marketing, that is excellent.

But when I wrote a sales letter to offer a service I did not believe in, I got nearly no replies. Why? The same writer created both letters. But my lack of belief in the second item was conveyed to people. They picked up on my vibe and "just knew" they better not order.

Another example is the flyer I received to attend a workshop in Seattle. All I saw was a dark photocopy of the original flyer. So I wasn't dazzled by bright colors, fancy type, clever copy or incredible graphics. But something about the flyer said "Sign up for this event." I did. When I spoke to others at the seminar, all of them said they had the same feeling. Many added, "I don't even know why I'm here. I saw the flyer and knew I was supposed to be here." The people who put on the seminar were clear about what they wanted. That confidence appeared in their brochures. And the people came.

Contrast that with a company I worked for at one time who wanted to put on a seminar about Internet marketing. This company was after only profits. There was no caring in their business and no sincere desire to serve people. That attitude showed up in their brochures. When they put on their event, they expected over two hundred people to attend. Only twenty people showed up.

I've noticed that many people have a negative attitude toward advertising. I think that's a limiting view. An ad can help you market your business. It can become another voice working on your behalf.

One day I was having dinner with Jerry and Esther Hicks and a friend. We were talking about marketing in general and advertising in particular. My friend said, "You don't have to advertise."

"You don't have to," I said, "but you might want to. A good ad can increase your business."

"The last time we ran an ad in a magazine," Jerry began, "we got so many replies we couldn't handle them all. I dropped the ad until we hired more staff."

"It doesn't matter what you put in the ad," Esther added. "People will sense who you are and what you are offering and make a decision from that feeling."

Jerry and Esther have hired me to write their ads because they know I believe in their work. If I didn't believe in them, the ads I create for them would show it. And if they didn't believe in their work, the person they hired to create their ads would reveal that attitude.

My friend Sandra Zimmer, who runs the Self-Expression Center in Houston, also knows the power of spiritually based advertising.

Sandra consciously infuses her ads with her energy. She actually sits and meditates over her ad, sending her energy into the ad. As a result, her ads have a magnetic quality to them. She once told me that people hold on to her ads for as long as seven years. I know I had seen Sandra's ads for many years, before I finally met her in person. While her ads didn't look different, they felt different. There was just something about her ads that made them memorable. That something was Sandra's own energy.

"Advertising is important," Sandra once told me. "But it's the energy you put in the ads that does the work. It's really the law of attraction at work."

Again, who you are inside creates the results you get outside. Even your marketing pieces carry your energy. Get clear, feel the energy of what you want to do, be or have, and you will naturally go in the direction of manifesting what you want.

When I was in Australia in May, 1999, I learned that many seeds don't open up and grow unless they are first burned.

In the human body, you open your seeds of desires with the heat of emotion. Whenever you feel love or fear, two very strong emotions, you are turning up the heat. That heat reaches your deeper mind and opens the seed, the image, of what you want. How you do that is through feeling.

The point of this step is that you must joyfully feel the energy of the thing you want to do, be, or have. As Joseph

Murphy wrote in his little book, *How to Attract Money,* "The feeling of wealth produces wealth."

Feel the joy of having what you want---feel it right now---and you will begin to pull it to you and you to it.

"The whole process of mental, spiritual and material riches may be summed up in one word: Gratitude."

-- *Your Infinite Power to be Rich* by Joseph Murphy, 1966

Step Five:
Let Go

Years ago I discovered that most of us, myself included, don't like to let go and allow because there's nothing for us to grapple with. There's no drama. Most of us feel that if we can't get in there and fight and struggle, we don't feel like we're accomplishing anything or getting anywhere. The struggle gives a sense of accomplishment. At least you can say, "Hey, I tried."

The ego gets a big rush out of struggle. The ego gets to feel that it is doing something worthwhile. Well, that's okay. If your ego needs a pat on the back, let it struggle for some of the things that you desire. But the truth is, you don't have to struggle at all. Again, it can be another way...an easier way.

I used to teach a class called "The Inner Game of Writing." It was modeled after the work of Tim Gallwey, who wrote *The Inner Game of Tennis* and co-authored several other "inner game" books. What I discovered was that we have at least two distinct beings within us, not personalities so much as aspects of our mind. Gallwey called it Self One and Self Two.

Self One can be likened to your ego, the part of you that wants to control.

Self Two can be likened to the inner master within you, the part of you that is connected to all things.

The job of Self One is to select what you want and let go. The job of Self Two is to bring it to you.

Gallwey learned that when people learned to let go and trust, they got what they wanted more often than not, and it came much easier than if they fought for it.

The same concept works in your life. Choose what you want and let God or the Universe (whatever that means to you) bring it to you. Let it orchestrate the events that will manifest the thing you desire. Give up needing to know how you will manifest anything. Knowing how can become a limitation. If you choose to manifest something but can't consciously see a way to create it, you may give up. The conscious mind can't see all of the possibilities. Surrender control and you free the universe to bring you whatever you want.

Tough to swallow? Then let me tell you a story...

When I was working on my book, *The Seven Lost Secrets of Success*, I was obsessed. I spent two years of my life on a mission to pay homage to Bruce Barton, a man who influenced our country but somehow fell through the cracks of history. One day I received a call from a medical Doctor in west Texas. He wanted to hire me to ghostwrite a book for him. While I was reluctant, going to see him felt like the right thing to do. I flew there, visited with him, negotiated a contract, and flew back to Houston with a large check in my hands, a nonrefundable retainer to hire me to write his book.

Weeks passed. Then months. During this time I spent most of my energy working on my Barton book. I rarely worked on the Doc's book, and never heard from him. I finally decided I should fly up to see him, and that I should present some material to him. So I made a flight reservation and started writing his book. But an odd thing happened. Whenever I called the Doctor's office, no one answered the phone. This went on for days. Then, a day before my flight was to leave, someone answered the phone. It was the Doc's business manager.

"Bill, this is Joe Vitale," I began.

"Hi Joe." His voice seemed sheepish.

"What's going on? No one has answered the phone there for days."

"Well, there's been a change in plans."

"What?"

Bill mumbled something. I asked him to repeat it. I couldn't believe what I heard.

"The Doc's in jail," he said.

To say I was stunned would be to lie. I was shocked. Speechless.

"The Doc's in jail!?!" I blurted. "Bill, what's going on?"

"Well, the Doc violated his parole."

Again I was shocked.

"You mean he's been in jail BEFORE?!"

"Well, the Doc sent a bomb to his ex-wife and he was caught and sent to prison," Bill explained. "He was allowed to come out and be a Doctor again but he couldn't play with guns or bombs anymore."

"Don't tell me," I said.

"Yea, they found bombs in his desk."

It took me a while to recover from this event. But I want you to notice the miracle here. When I signed a contract with the Doctor, I was given a large sum of money. Non-refundable money. Money that enabled me to work on my Barton book. And then, when the Doctor went to jail, I was free from his contract. I didn't have to write his book at all.

Somehow God or the Universe (or whatever you want to call the invisible powers that be) set the stage for this grand event. Could I have orchestrated such an event? It's highly unlikely. How would I have written the ad?

"Doctor wanted: Must be ex-con, want to write a book, and be ready to go back to jail in six months so I can keep his money."

I don't think so.

Again, when you know what you want and are clear, you will be drawn to the thing you want and events will pull it to you. Jonathan sees this happen all the time. When two Doctors in Seattle couldn't agree on office space they needed, they went to Jonathan. After one session they were clear. Within twenty-four hours they found the space they needed, and signed a lease for it.

I saw the same thing happen when my wife and I wanted to buy a house. If you are trying to manifest something that involves another person, both of you have to be clear before you'll manifest the event. I had worked on myself to buy the house I wanted. But things still weren't working out. Finally my wife went to see Jonathan. She cleared up some old beliefs she had about self-worth and money. The very next day the real estate people called. Three days later we moved into the house. And this was after nearly twelve months of delays!

Would you like an example from the world of business?

Dan Poynter is a dear friend and internationally recognized expert on self-publishing. He's written several books, including the famous *Self-Publishing Manual*. Dan also conducts weekend seminars in his home on how to self-publish and market your own book. He's been offering this seminar for over ten years, has helped hundreds of people, but has always struggled to get people to register for the event. One day Dan called me for my help.

"Joe, I want you to write a brochure for me that is so powerful that people sign up for my seminar without my having to do a thing."

Notice what Dan was doing. He knew what he didn't want (to pull teeth to get people to come to his seminar) and he knew what he did want (to have people call and register easily and effortlessly). From those two steps he was led to calling me. When I agreed to create a new brochure for Dan, what did he have to do?

Let go.

He had to let go. He had to trust that he hired the right guy and all would be well. While he didn't know it, "letting go" is a key step in the manifestation process. He was intuitively following it.

I designed a flyer for Dan, he loved it, and he printed it. A few weeks later I called him and he said, "My seminar is already sold out."

"It is?!" I yelled, delighted. But Dan stopped me in my tracks.

"But it isn't due to your flyer," he said.

"It isn't?"

"The seminar sold out two weeks ago and I only last week mailed out the new flyer. There had been a delay in the mailing."

"Then what happened?" I asked. "Why did it sell out?"

Dan didn't know. But here's my guess: As you know by now, the energy you give out brings the results you get. When Dan stated his new intention, and allowed me to create a new flyer for him, he was changing the inner signal he was sending it. Once you change the way you are inside, the outer world changes. Dan didn't even have to mail his flyer out. People picked up on the signals in the air and responded.

Crazy? Maybe so. But as I've pointed out throughout this book, the energy you give out attracts and creates the results you get. Change your inner energy and you change your results.

(And for the record, I later saw Dan in Chicago, where he told me that due to my new brochure for him, his August seminar sold out in the previous JUNE.)

The following story reveals how my latest (and in many ways greatest) dream just came true. I am sharing it with you in the hope that it inspires you to go for your own dreams. It's all about the power of setting an intention and then letting go of it...

If you've never seen the famous Nightingale-Conant giant catalog of audiotapes on business, motivation, self-help, relationships, health and spirituality, reach over to your phone right now and call 1-800-525-9000. Or visit their site at http://www.nightingale.com. Request the catalog. It's free and well worth browsing.

I wanted to have a tapeset of my own in the Nightingale-Conant catalog for many years. I wanted it for the prestige, as well as for the profit. I wanted to be among their roster of greats: Tony Robbins, Tom Peters, Deepak Chopra, Bob Proctor, Joe Vitale, Brian Tracy, and Wayne Dyer.

But until Autumn, 1998, this desire had only been a dream. Despite the fact that I always sent Nightingale-Conant my new books as soon as they were published, I could never seem to ignite their interest in my work.

But I never gave up. I simply held onto the dream, trusted that something would give sooner or later, and kept doing my thing: Writing what I hoped were inspiring and informative books.

And then something amazing happened.

One day a man began sending me e-mail, asking numerous questions about marketing in general and P.T. Barnum in particular. He was a fan of Barnum's and loved my book, *There's a Customer Born Every Minute.* I answered all of his questions, glad to help.

Then one day I received a shock. The man sent me e-mail saying, "If you ever want your material considered by Nightingale-Conant, let me know. I'm their Marketing Project Manager."

You can't imagine my surprise. Or my delight.

I immediately Fed-Xed all of my books, my video, and my home study course (six audiotapes and a workbook) to my new friend at Nightingale-Conant. He didn't like anything I sent. Instead, he LOVED everything I sent. And right then and there he began the long process of selling Nightingale-Conant on me.

After eleven months of calls, faxes, and many Fed-X's, I am proud to announce that Nightingale-Conant is carrying

Joe Vitale

their first product by me. It's called "The Power of Outrageous Marketing."

This amazing story illustrates many lessons:

...The power of a dream (I held my vision of what I wanted for years).

...The networking potential of the Internet (My Nightingale-Conant contact found me at my website).

...The miracle that comes from having someone who believes in you. (My contact believes in me to a staggering degree, and told me so over and over again for eleven months.)

...The true magic that occurs when you are in alignment with your life's purpose and doing what makes your heart sing...

...And the power of letting go.

And I'm sure there are other lessons in this story, lessons that you see and I don't. Again, I am sharing this with you in the hope that it sets your own heart on fire, awakens something in your soul, and urges you to go for---and get---your own dreams.

And here's something else to think about:

According to research done at Spindrift Foundation on the power of prayer, a "Thy will be done" prayer gets more than twice as many results as a specific "give me this" prayer. That's why it's so important to end your request for anything you want with the magic words, "This or something better."

When I was writing my book on P.T. Barnum, I went to the famous showman's grave in Bridgeport, Connecticut. I had a moving experience there, which I wrote about in my book. But what I want to share with you here is what I saw written on Barnum's gravesite marker. To my surprise, carved in his simple concrete headstone were these magical words, words that Barnum relied on throughout his colorful life:

"Not my will but thine be done."

Those magic words worked for Barnum, helping him to survive personal and professional disasters, and helping him become one of America's first millionaires, and those words can work for you, too.

In other words, trust the universe.

109

You can ask for whatever you want to do, be, or have, but also be willing for the universe to give you something better. End all of your requests with the phrase, "This or something better" and you will be letting the universe know that "Thy will be done" is of highest importance.

Why is this so? Because the universe can see the big picture while your ego can't.

Your job is to ask for what you want, and then to act on the inner nudges you get to do things, like make phone calls, write letters, visit a certain person, or whatever. Bob Proctor, in his wonderful book, *You Were Born Rich*, puts it this way:

"Learn to follow the quiet voice within that speaks in feelings rather than words; follow what you 'hear' inside, rather than what others may be telling you to do."

The universe itself will act to move you to what you want, and move what you want to you. All you have to do is let go, while acting on your inner prompts. Let go of fear, doubt, worry, disappointment, and any other negative emotion that might make you feel low.

The famous poet and sage Rumi wrote something that may help you here:

"Some things that don't happen keep disasters from happening."

Think about it. What you're being asked to do is trust. Trust that when something happens, it's good; and trust that when something you want doesn't happen, it's good, too.

Here's one final story on the subject of letting go...

I attended Bob Proctor's three day course called The Science of Getting Rich in Denver during June of 1999. It was a mind-expanding experience. I urge you to take the course live if at all possible, or at least to invest in the home-study course. There are so many things you'll get out of the material that where you are now will seem like poverty after you absorb the materials and become wealthy.

But one idea that I got from Bob's course that I want to give you right now is this quote:

"Everything that happens in your life is moving you in the direction of your goals."

Now think about this. That statement says that everything, without fail, without exception, is moving you toward your dreams.

So if something happens that you feel is bad, remember that it happened to move you forward. Your job is to find the positive in the negative, or at least to trust that there is a positive there, even if you can't see it at the moment.

This might be tough to accept, at first. But the truth is, it is an enlightened way of living your life. I love the statement and thank Bob Proctor for saying it. What it tells me is that I have to let go and trust that life itself is taking me to the things I desire.

And as I let go, trust, and give thanks for my life, I feel different, I radiant a different vibration to the world, and better things and experiences come to me.

Again, the whole secret is in learning to simply let go.

"Everything that happens in your life is moving you in the direction of your goals."

Bob Proctor

The Million Dollar Formula

"What's the hardest part to creating life the way you want it?" a friend asked me over lunch.

I thought for a moment and replied, "Learning to stop figuring out how you will get what you want."

My friend looked confused.

She asked, "What do you mean?"

"If you try to figure out how you will get that new car, or that new house, or that new relationship, you'll limit yourself to what your ego can see and do," I explained. "Turn your goal over to your unconscious, which is connected to the spirit of everything and everyone, and let it bring the goal to you and you to the goal. Just follow your inner promptings and act on the opportunities that come your way, and you'll get there."

Well, I'm not sure if my friend understood what I was saying. But a few days later I was sitting in a limousine, being driven to have dinner with eight wealthy, wonderful, self-made people. All of these people started with nothing. Many of them started as I had: With empty pockets and hope in their hearts.

As I sat in the limo, a part of me couldn't believe I was there.

"How did I get here?" I remember thinking to myself. "I'm in a beautiful limo, with beautiful people beside me, going to have a beautiful dinner that some other beautiful person is going to pay for. I'm just a nobody kid from Ohio who left home to find fame and fortune. I used to dig ditches, drive trucks, work in the dirt, the rain, and the heat, and for never enough money to pay my bills. How'd I get in this limo?"

As I thought about it, I knew the secret was the five step formula I've revealed to you in this book. In short, the secret to increasing your business or manifesting whatever you want is:

1. Know what you don't want.

2. Select what you do want.

3. Clear all negative or limiting beliefs.

4. Feel what it would be like to have, do, or be what you want.

5. Let go. Act on your intuitive impulses and allow the results to manifest.

Truth is, there's no "one way" to achieve anything in this world. Some people get new cars by winning them, others by struggling to pay for them, others by happily paying for them, others by other means. What I told my friend at lunch is the truth: You can't orchestrate the world to do your bidding. Instead, state your intentions and let the world arrange itself to bring your goals to you.

I was in that limo because I didn't plan to be in it.

I allowed, acted, trusted, and accepted.

I followed the five-step formula.

And when the limo pulled up, I got in.

Finally, I can't find any better way of ending this book then with this quote from Frances Larimer Warner, written in 1907. When I was interviewed on a late night talk show one evening, they asked me to read this quote to them twice. Then they were silent for a moment while the meaning of these words hit home.

I'll end this book with those same words, and wish you "God speed" in making all your dreams come true.

And when your limo pulls up, get in!

"If we plant a seed in the ground we know that the sun will shine and the rain will water, and we leave it to the Law to bring results...Well, the desire you image is the seed, your occasional closing of the eyes in imagery is the sun, and your constant, though not anxious, expectation is the rain and cultivation necessary to bring absolutely sure results..."

-- Frances Larimer Warner, *Our Invisible Supply: Part One*
1907

"What happened to Jonathan?"

Nearly every day I get a call, an email, or a letter from someone asking—

"What happened to Jonathan?"

Every person asking the question read this book, marveled at the stories of my miraculous (and even shocking) work with Jonathan, and now wants to meet the man himself.

The thing is, Jonathan is no longer available. He has taken time off to do personal things.

Meanwhile, my adventures continue and my life is one of magic and miracles. How do I stay clear and focused? I work with several people these days to keep myself on track. Most of them are listed in the back of this book.

Ann Taylor Harcus is the person I've been working with most recently. I first heard of her because of her ad in New Age Journal. Her ad has a "magnetic charge" to it.

The ad said she heals people on a cellular level. She has helped more than 10,000 people, so far. She's endorsed by Dr. Bernie Siegel. The ad went on to list some of the problems she has helped people release: Health issues, money problems, allergies, anger, fear, relationship issues...there's an impressive list in the ad. It almost sounds too good to be true.

But the add also says you can have a free 15-minute phone consultation with her, to get a sense of her work. I called, met Ann by phone, and have been working with her ever since.

If you want to work with someone to help you achieve your dreams, I offer Ann. Her website is at http://www.innerhealing.com. Her email is

118

Miracles22@aol.com. Her phone is 1-816-478-0722 or toll-free 1-888-816-7822.

Suggested Reading and Listening

Books and tapes can keep your mind focused on the positive and help you keep going toward your dreams. The following are my suggestions for extra fun. I've only listed the books that are still in print. With a little searching you can also find countless other wonderful books, now out of print, to keep your inner fires stoked. Just pick whatever title calls to you and enjoy it. As you complete that book, you'll be led to others. Relish the journey, my friend! You're in for a treat!

Dr. Robert Anthony's Advanced Formula For Total Success by Dr. Robert Anthony. This 1988 no-nonsense little gem surprised me by being so inspiring, practical, and akin to the ideas expressed here in my own book. Anthony has written several other books, all worth getting. Order online at www.amazon.com.

Joe Vitale

The Magic of Believing by Claude Bristol. My all-time favorite on the power of using your mind to create anything you want. It's been in print since 1948. I first read it when I was a teenager. A masterpiece. At bookstores or order from http://www.amazon.com

The Emergency Handbook for Getting Money Fast! is an incredible book by Carole Dore. This uplifting book reveals an "inside out" approach to making money. What Doré reveals are strategic ways to increase your energy so that money is literally drawn to you like a magnet. Order it by FAX (949) 857-5122 or call 1-800-40-POWER.

Feelings Buried Alive Never Die... by Karol Truman. Reveals a powerful one-step process for releasing the core issues in your life so you can be clear to have what you want. Brilliant. Order online at http://www.healing-hearts.com or call 1-800-531-3180.

Keys to the Ultimate Freedom by Lester Levenson, founder of the Sedona Method, a very simple way to "get clear" so you can become Master of your life. This book

120

contains Lester's thoughts about life, which are illuminating. Call 1-888-282-5656. Or visit http://www.sedona.com.

The Power of Outrageous Marketing!, an audiotape program, with workbook, by Joe Vitale. Teaches you the ten proven secrets for fame, fortune, and immortality. From Nightingale-Conant. Call 1-800-525-9000 or visit http://www.nightingale.com.

The Power of Your Subconscious Mind by Dr. Joseph Murphy. Anything by Murphy is worth reading. This is a classic. Available in most bookstores or online at http://www.amazon.com

Sara and the Foreverness of Friends of a Feather by Jerry and Esther Hicks. A delightful work of fiction which teaches how to make your own world through the science of deliberate creation. Call (830) 755-2299. Visit http://www.abraham-hicks.com

The Science of Getting Rich by Bob Proctor. This is a stunning course (book, workbook, and eight tapes), based on the 1903 book by Wallace Wattles, on using your mind to increase your wealth. If you only wanted to get one book out of the list here, this would be the one. Call 1-800-871-9715. Or visit http://www.bobproctor.com

The Seven Lost Secrets of Success by Joe Vitale. Now in it's seventh edition and still changing the world, one person at a time. Reveals the marketing secrets of a forgotten genius from the roaring twenties. One company bought 19,500 copies of this book. Visit http://www.amazon.com to order.

So, Why Aren't You Rich? If you want to read a book to rattle your cage, pick up a copy of Darel Rutherford's nuclear blast to the ego. It's billed as the unauthorized sequel to Napoleon Hill's famous book, "Think and Grow Rich." Get more details, and sign up for Darel's free e-newsletter, at http://www.richbits.com

Spiritual Economics: The Principles and Process of True Prosperity by Eric Butterworth. A Unity minister's insights into wealth. Outstanding. At bookstores, or call 1-800-669-0282, or order online at http://www.amazon.com

Ten Thousand Whispers: A Guide to Conscious Creation by Lynda Madden Dahl. Mind-expanding. Also read her book, *Beyond the Winning Streak*. Order from http://www.amazon.com or call (541) 683-0803.

Travelling Free by Mandy Evans. A petite guide on how your beliefs create your reality, and how to change your beliefs through a gentle questioning process. Call 1-800-356-9315 or order online at http://www.amazon.com

Working with the Law by Dr. Raymond Holliwell. Reveals the laws of the universe. Work with them and you can have whatever your heart desires. Call 1-800-871-9715.

You Were Born Rich by Bob Proctor. An incredible book on how to unlock your potential. Available as a home-study course, too. Call 1-800-871-9715. Or visit http://www.bobproctor.com

Joe Vitale

Healers, Mentors, and Counselors

Ann Taylor Harcus	miracles22@aol.com
Bill Ferguson	wff@neosoft.com
Kathy DeMont	remoteheal@hotmail.com
Mandy Evans	beliefs@mandyevans.com
Karol Truman	feelings@infowest.com
Diana Bay	Mehob@aol.com
Merry Mount	merrymount@earthlink.net
Gloriana Ron Da	RonDahTherapies@aol.com

Printed in the United States
27696LVS00001B/169-237